TODAY WAS MY FIRST CELLO LESSON

WRITTEN AND ILLUSTRATED BY RAFAEL RAMIREZ

DIGITALIZED BY NORMAN BERMUDEZ

EDITED BY MARIA A. BERMUDEZ

©2014 Rafael Ramirez

Hi, my name is Christian.

Today was my first cello lesson.

My Mom told me that I will learn how to play the cello.
We went to my teacher's Cello Studio.

Mr. Ramirez is my cello teacher.

My teacher told me about

the different parts of the cello...

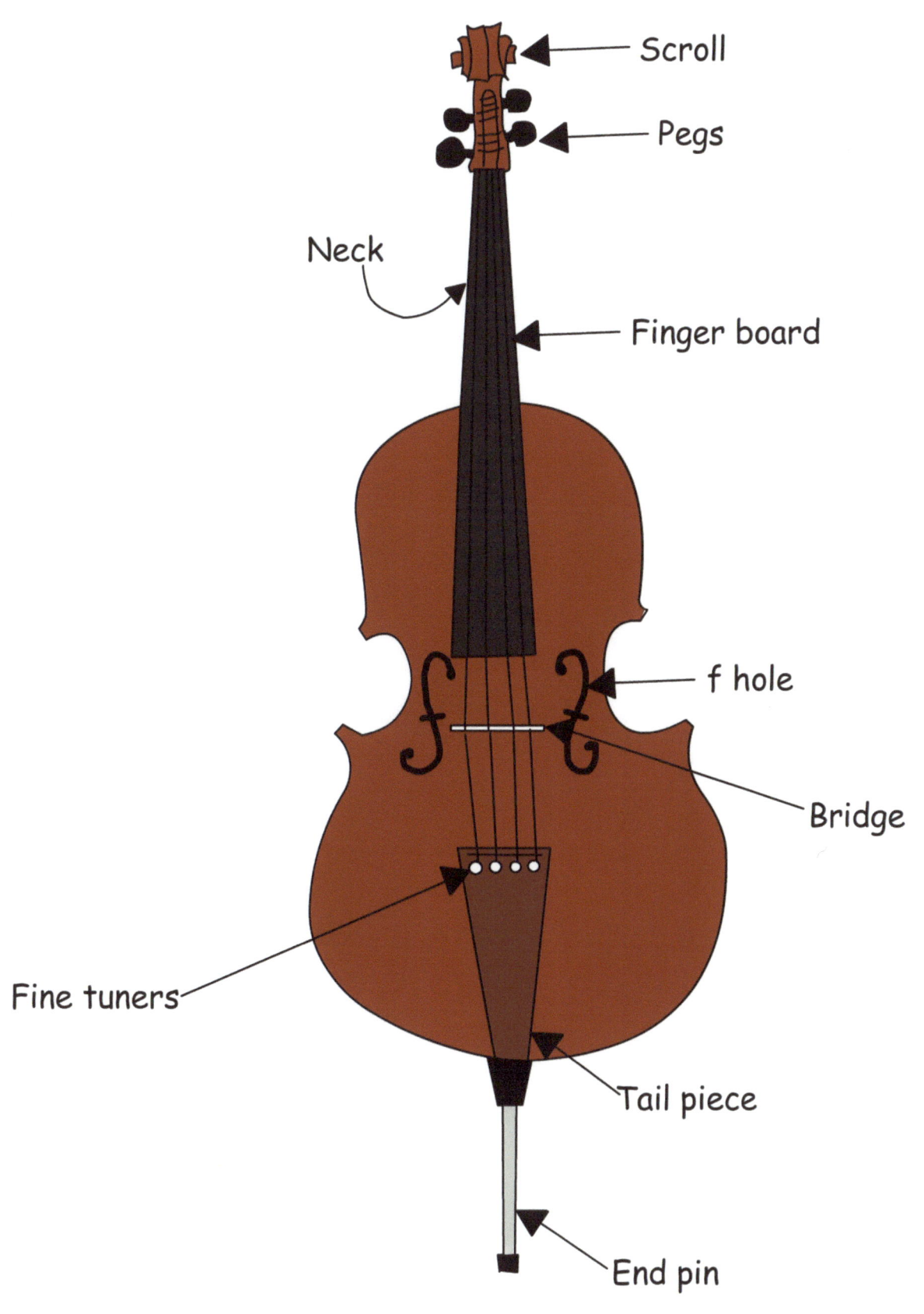

...And

the parts of the bow.

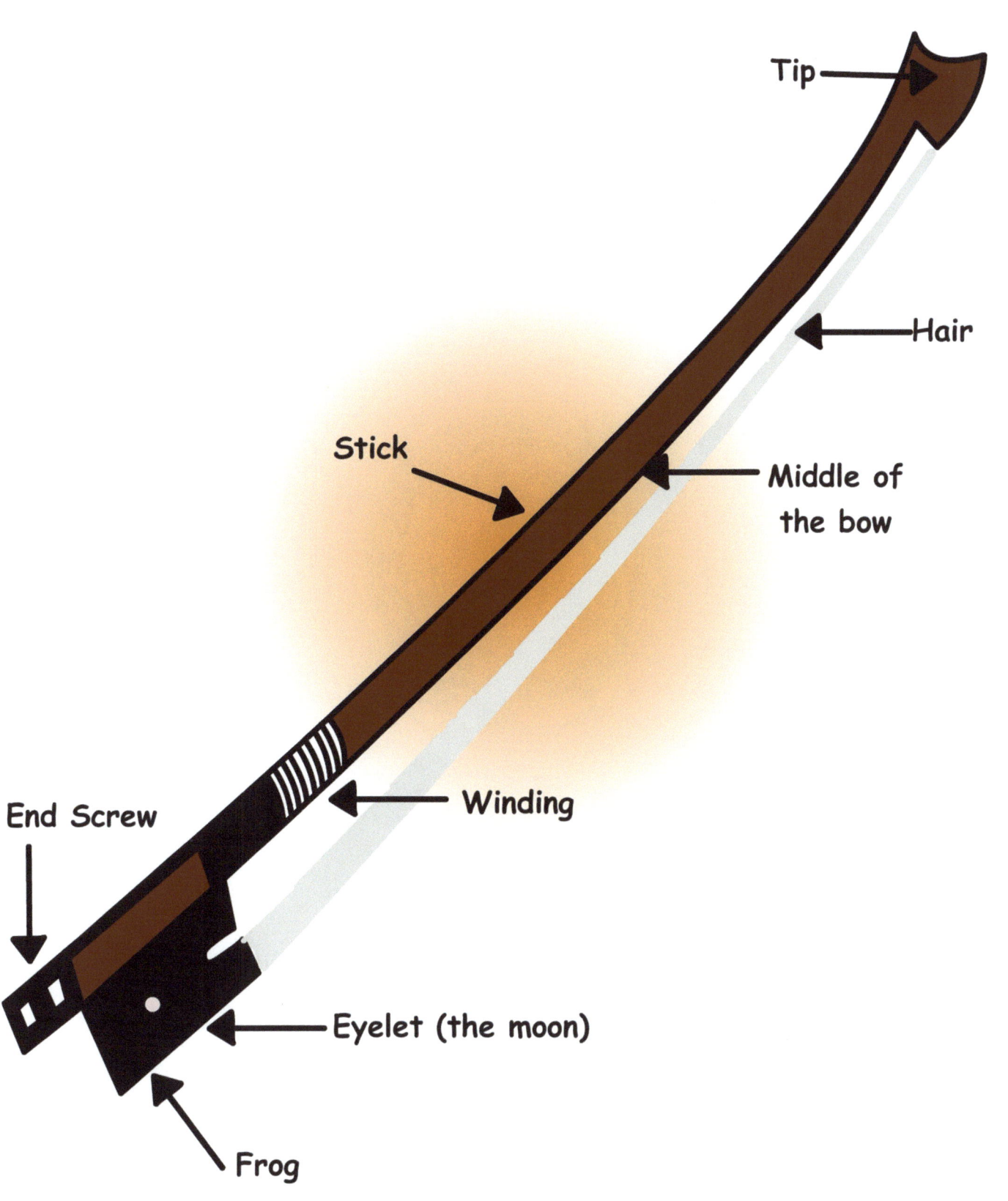

I need to practice how to hold the bow. This will help me make a beautiful sound.

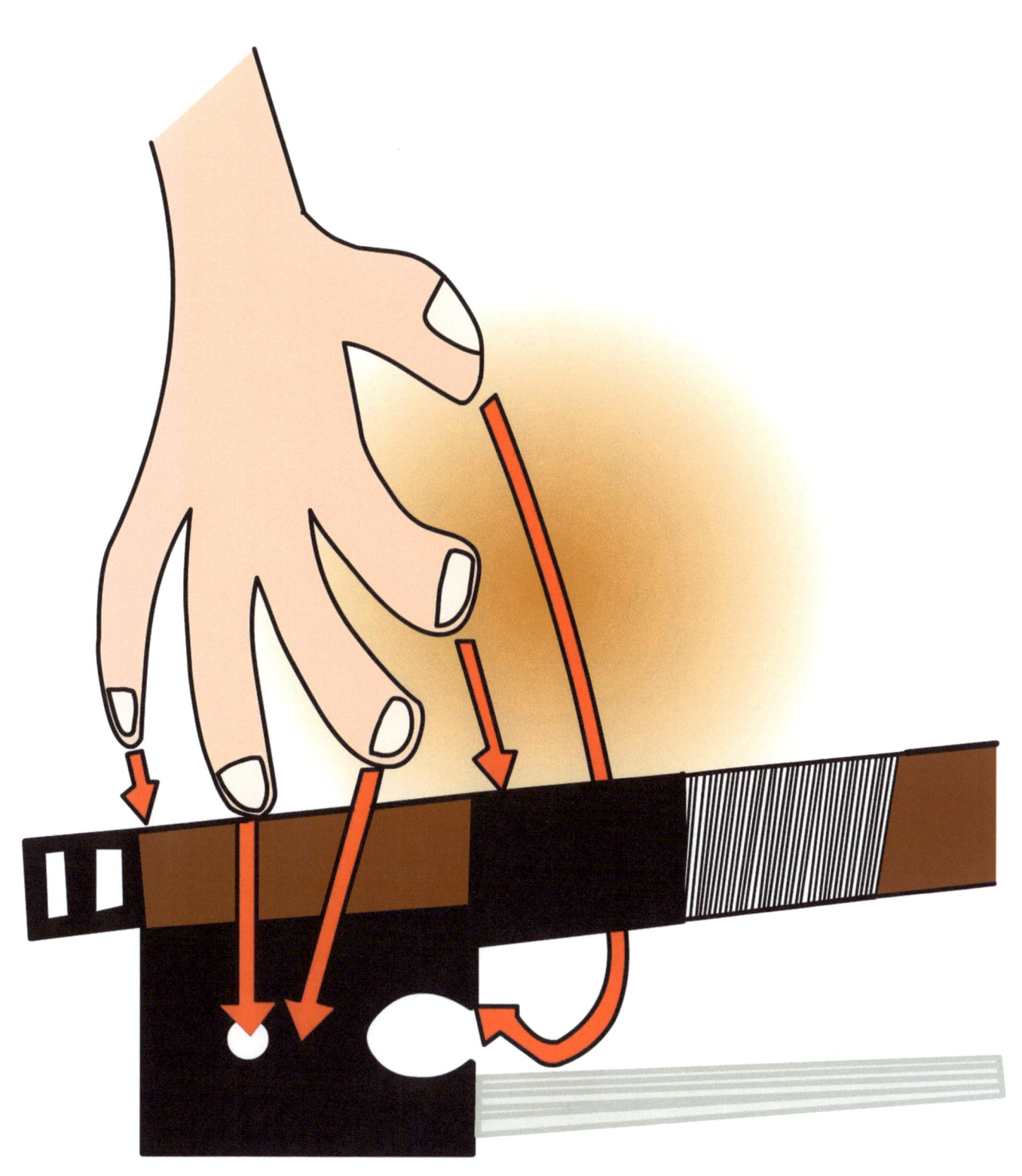

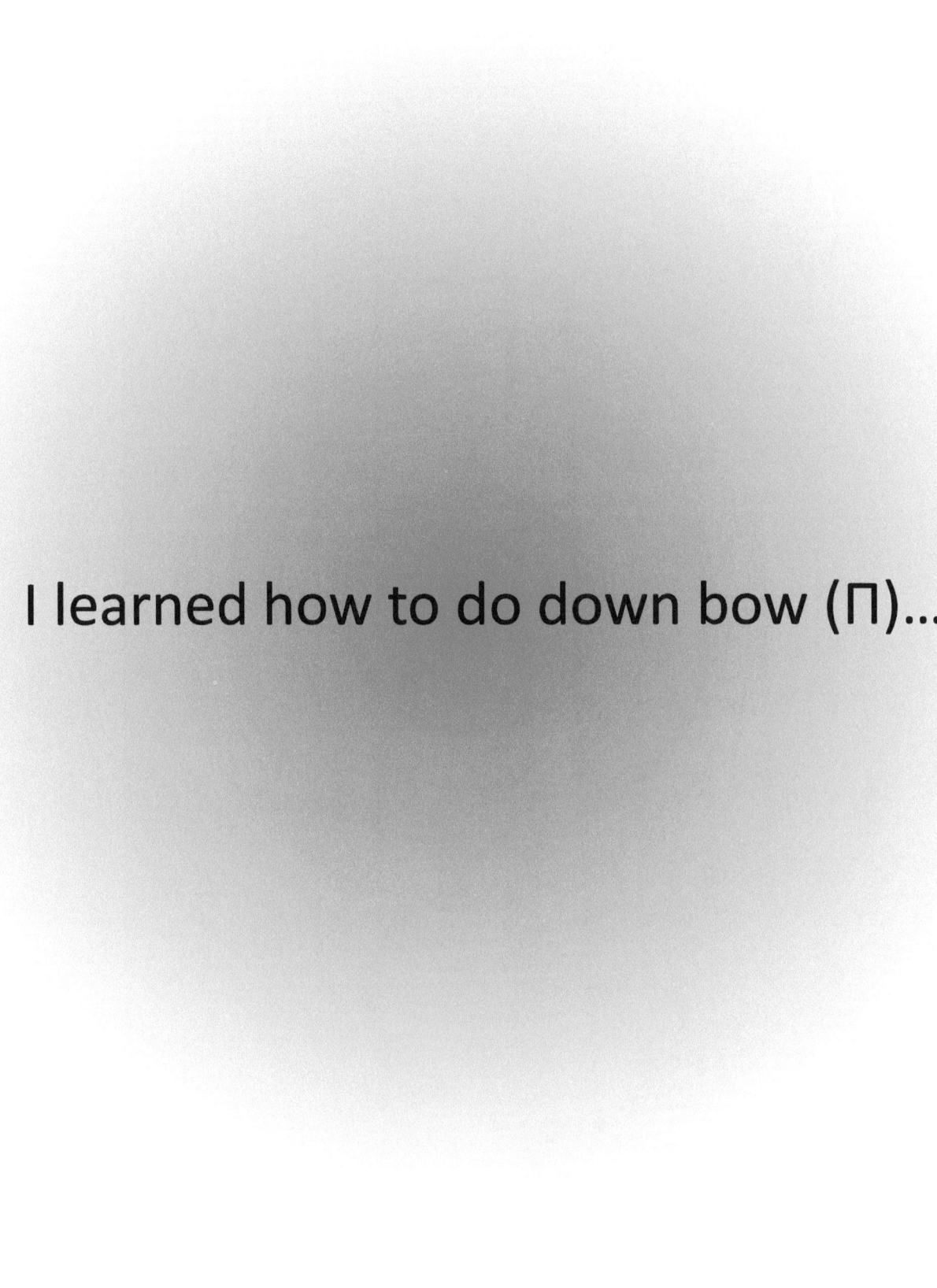

I learned how to do down bow (Π)...

...and up bow (V).

Mr. Ramirez said:

"The bow has to go straight like a train to make a beautiful sound."

I learned about:

The music staff. It is used to notate music.

The pitches — The musical notes, and the type of notes.

Today was my first cello lesson and I had fun.

My teacher surprised me at the end of the lesson with a piece of candy and my first cello book.

Playing the cello is cool.

I love it!

www.ingramcontent.com/pod-product-compliance
Lightning Source LLC
Chambersburg PA
CBHW041232040426
42444CB00002B/133